I0440344

HALLSTATT PICTURE BOOK

Capturing the Charm and Beauty of Hallstatt in a Stunning Picture Book (High quality photos)

Bonita Green

Amazing photos of Hallstatt

VPBank

ELEGANT RESIDENCES
212.
684.
3222

REALTOR BUIL
ULTA

2019

ORIENTA

Travel Planner

Destination (s)	When

Expenses	Budget	Actual

Transport ation		
Hotel		
Food		
Shopping		
Gifts		

Total		

Places to see

Places to eat

- ____________________

Places to shop

- ____________________
- ____________________
- ____________________
- ____________________
- ____________________

Emergency contacts

- ______________________________
- ______________________________
- ______________________________
- ______________________________
- ______________________________

Addresses of places I'm staying at

- ______________________________
- ______________________________
- ______________________________
- ______________________________

www.ingramcontent.com/pod-product-compliance
Lightning Source LLC
Chambersburg PA
CBHW041826280526
45792CB00006B/2008
* 9 7 9 8 8 6 7 2 3 4 4 0 9 *